"Mark Blackshear is a gift from God to this generation. In *Game Over*, Mark brilliantly yet simply displays The Gospel's power to change lives. I highly recommend that youth and youth leaders read this book!"

–Victor Schloss, Religious Studies, SDSUExt. Faculty

"Mark has written a guide that meets young people struggling with addiction right where they're at—but doesn't just leave them there."

-James Fazio, Th.M. Dean of Students at Southern California Seminary

"I have spent more than a decade hoping to weave a plan that would motivate young souls toward a desire for substance abuse recovery. Mark has taken the core of his inspirational heart and his understanding of God's healing power and created a manual that inspires such a desire for deliverance from the crippling condition caused by drug and alcohol abuse."

-Debra Hullaby, Registered Addiction Specialist and Founder of Victory in Behavioral Education

"Game over Youth Substance Abuse Manual", by Mark Blackshear offers a timely solution for therapists, counselors, parents, clergy and other providers who are concerned about a young person who might be headed in a wrong direction as a result of their substance abuse. This manual offers practical solutions and a clear path to recovery. I strongly recommend it and I applaud Mark for his personal story and his much needed contribution towards the health and wellness of our young people."

-Roland Williams, MA, LAADC, CADCII, NCACII, SAP, President and Founder, Free Life Enterprises and VIP Recovery Coaching

GAME OVER:

A Youth Substance Abuse Manual

MARK BLACK

WESTBOW
PRESS®
A DIVISION OF THOMAS NELSON
& ZONDERVAN

WestBow Press books may be ordered through booksellers or by contacting:

WestBow Press
A Division of Thomas Nelson & Zondervan
1663 Liberty Drive
Bloomington, IN 47403
www.westbowpress.com
844-714-3454

Scriptures taken from the Holy Bible, New International Version®, NIV®.
Copyright © 1973, 1978, 1984, 2011 by Biblica, Inc.™ Used by permission
of Zondervan. All rights reserved worldwide. www.zondervan.com The
"NIV" and "New International Version" are trademarks registered in
the United States Patent and Trademark Office by Biblica, Inc.™
All rights reserved.

ISBN: 978-1-4908-1191-8 (sc)
ISBN: 978-1-4908-1192-5 (hc)
ISBN: 978-1-4908-1190-1 (e)

Library of Congress Control Number: 2013918556

Print information available on the last page.

WestBow Press rev. date: 02/23/2021

TABLE OF CONTENTS

ACKNOWLEDGMENTS

Thank You, Jesus, for giving Your life so that we may have eternal life. Thanks to Pastor Miles, Pastor Terrell, and Pastor Vic for inspiring young leaders. My gratitude to; my Father, my Mother, DeDe, Nina, Dezzy, Dixie Crane, Exton and Debra Hullaby, my church family; and my accountability partners new and old, especially Ashton and Franklin.

INTRODUCTION

When I was fifteen, I remember pretending to spend the night at friends' houses, only to drink and escape my personal issues secretly. I remember finishing my first six-pack of beer and then moving into hard liquor, marijuana, and mushrooms at age sixteen. I was a kid with a high tolerance at such a young age, and by the time I turned eighteen, I was a young alcoholic and a chronic smoker who sold drugs to be "cool." But it all ended in a single night. After several near-death experiences and run- ins with the police in America and in Mexico, I stood at gunpoint and was left with a choice to make—life or death.

At age nineteen, I chose life abundantly, and immediately my life began to change for the better. I found that I was sent to guide and work with kids who had lived lives like mine. Now, after nineteen years of working with youth in various settings, from camps to group homes to faith- based organizations to nonprofits, I have come to find that substance abuse remains a bleak commonality throughout adolescence. For these severely emotionally disturbed children and at-risk teens, the number one coping mechanism is drugs and alcohol.

On my way toward becoming a drug and alcohol counselor, serving in several capacities as a group and individual substance abuse counselor, I have found the typical counselor approach to be intertwined with client and counselor dependence. However, I have seen and personally experienced "independent treatment", "self-actualization" or "self- help," dozens of time. Over the years, I have observed that self-help is more effective than drug treatment, and the success rates of staying clean and sober through self-help are much higher in those I have counseled than those in treatment.

I pose this question to you: Can youth recover from substance abuse on their own? The concern is that many substance abuse counselors will tell you no even when the evidence suggests that yes, young people are capable of this. This guide aims to prove the latter, demonstrating that the youth of today are capable of growth and change in the midst of recovery.

This book was created forthe post millennial generation who are scanning their mental and physical health, friendships, environments, cultural influences, and their spiritual maturity for a glimpse of freedom from drugs and alcohol. Most young people are anxious to make strides down the path of change; all they need is illumination on their way.

WELCOME

It's out. Your secret. Everyone knows: your friends, your parents, your brothers and sisters, your teachers, your classmates, your significant other. They all know you have a problem. You've tried to mask it behind quick restroom encounters with Visine, behind your lies, behind your chilled attitude and your cracked smile. But now everyone sees it. Your secret is in plain sight. Like the heat rising from hot asphalt, we can see the abuse you have done to your body. The abuse gripped like fingertips to sparked matches and you tried to blow it out, only the harder you blew, the quicker it burned and the quicker the light in your life began to get darker. If there was ever a time you thought you had this locked away, the game is over.

No longer can you assume that they don't know. No longer can you mask your innocence with perfumes and cologne. It is time to get up out of the darkness. Put that shame down and walk into a new sunrise. You didn't give in to defeat; you merely postponed your victory. These words are sent to capture you back from within, to sweep you toward a better place. You might have thought you could quit at any time, but you can't dig your way out of a young addict's hole. Today is the day you give it up for good. But you must first get up, admit your mistakes, and come to terms with the fact that the game is over.

Game Over is to be read one day at a time. No more and no less. Each lesson is to be reflected upon, practiced, and shared. Congratulations on choosing to end the game on your substance abuse!

DAY 1

It's a miracle that you're reading this book. I should have died on three occasions. Since I was eighteen years old, I have watched my childhood friends die one by one. First I began to see them as walking obituaries on T-shirts. I remember how my heart felt the first time I saw my boy resting in peace on a T-shirt. My heart dropped into my stomach, and all the memories I had of him flashed before my eyes. It was a shock to see that someone I was just making plans with had been killed. I think that was when I began to drink to mask the pain of losing close friends. They looked like me, they had the same interests, we ran in the same circles, and we got caught in the same situations. My thoughts would echo: *That bullet was for me.*

Out of my group of childhood friends I grew up with, I am the only one alive and free. One was shot dead, and two are incarcerated for life. I was only one choice away from joining them. But my life has been spared. Why? Perhaps I was sent here to share a truth with you. Perhaps my life was spared to be an example, or perhaps I am still here to show the way to those who are going through the challenges I did.

I was high the first time I almost lost my life. We spent the entire afternoon blazing. As we made our way home, I stopped at Jack in

1

the Box, a usual high-time ritual. As I grabbed my chicken sandwich, we pulled away, forgetting the ranch dressing. I got to my room and killed it!

I remember being so high that I could not feel the food going down my throat, much less chewing it. Sure enough, I bit off more than I could chew. A three-inch chunk of chicken lodged in my throat, and I began to gasp for air. Alone in my room, I could not yell. As my need for air increased, my eyes and throat began to swell with blood looking for oxygen. My life flashed before my eyes. Death had a subtle sting. It felt as if my soul was being pulled out of my body, and I went to a dark place. Completely numb, I fell over and hit the floor, with my elbow tucked across my chest. I was dead. No life, no breath, no thoughts. Just darkness.

After a minute or so, I began to cough up something horrible. The impact from hitting the floor must have knocked the food out of my windpipe. This was my first warning from God. Looking back at that moment in my life, I needed to take a self-inventory.

Those furthest from the temptations of drugs and alcohol have no immediate family or health concerns regarding drug or alcohol abuse. They have no behavior problems at school or in society. They know how to say no and how to handle stressful situations without taking substances. They enjoy life, friends, relationships, and school. They spend time with their families and with God, and they practice staying away from substances each and every day.

But for the rest of us, the *Game Over* Self-Inventory determines what areas need improvement and what areas cannot be changed. Self-Inventory gives us a unique perspective of our strengths, weaknesses, opportunities, and threats. It also addresses how we react and think when confronted with substance abuse. Successful recovery from substance abuse requires self-inventory first. The *Game Over* Self-Inventory is modeled after the Teen Addiction Severity Index, the SWOT Analysis, Alcohol Use Disorders Identification Test, CAGE Test, TWEAK Test, and the CRAFFT Questionnaire.

Ask yourself where you see drug abuse and alcoholism playing a role in your life, paying special attention to these categories.

1. Family health and drug history
2. Behaviors and stressors
3. Friends and social networks
4. Schools and neighborhoods
5. Family and traditions
6. Faith and religion

Begin.

Game Over Self-Inventory

Example:

1	2	3	5	Scenario:
Never	Sometimes	Often	Always	I have seen my parents use drugs or get drunk.

| ☐ | ☐ | ☐ | ☒ | |

Biological: Health & Family Drug & Alcohol History

☐	☐	☐	☐	My parent(s) use or have used drugs.
☐	☐	☐	☐	My parent(s) get drunk.
☐	☐	☐	☐	My parent(s) argue or have argued.
☐	☐	☐	☐	My family members encourage my drug usage & my drinking.
☐	☐	☐	☐	My parent(s) is very strict or controlling.
☐	☐	☐	☐	My family argues with me about my drug or alcohol usage.
☐	☐	☐	☐	My family member abuses me after they have gotten high or drunk.
☐	☐	☐	☐	I use or get drunk because it helps me do better in life.
☐	☐	☐	☐	I use or get drunk to deal with my mental health concerns.
☐	☐	☐	☐	I use or get drunk to deal with my sleep issues.

Totals each column				
				Grand Total:

4

SCORE INTERPRETATION_____

0–10: Low Exposure. Your family hardly ever drinks or uses substances in front of you. Your psychological factors for using are at low levels.

11–20: Minimal Exposure. Your family sometimes drinks or uses substances in front of you. If their behavior is not looked at as negative, you could be in the same position as them soon.

21–30: Moderate Exposure. Your family often uses and drinks in front of you. It may be hard for you to turn down drugs and alcohol because you have observed them to be a part of life. Your focus should shift to positive activities outside of your home.

31–50: Major Exposure. You are in a bad situation. Talk with a school counselor or school nurse about your home situation. You may want to live with a close relative who does not use or drink.

Example:

1	2	3	5	Scenario:
Never	Sometimes	Often	Always	I have seen my parents use drugs or get drunk.
☐	☐	☐	☒	

Psychological: Behavior & Coping Skills

☐	☐	☐	☐	I feel more stable when I use or get drunk.
☐	☐	☐	☐	Drugs and alcohol get me in trouble.
☐	☐	☐	☐	I have trouble sleeping so I use or drink to fall asleep.
☐	☐	☐	☐	I would rather use or drink then stay out of trouble.
☐	☐	☐	☐	I have suicidal thoughts.
☐	☐	☐	☐	I constantly sleep with other people.
☐	☐	☐	☐	I can only sleep with other people when I am high or drunk.
☐	☐	☐	☐	I have a previously diagnosed issue.
☐	☐	☐	☐	I have a to get high or drunk in order to fall asleep.
☐	☐	☐	☐	I use or drink in order to forget.

Totals each column				
				Grand Total:

SCORE INTERPRETATION_____

0–10: Low Exposure. You rarely/never drink or use. Your mental health is strong.

11–20: Minimal Exposure. You sometimes have a drink or get high. You may not want to, but you find yourself using or drinking. Now is a good time to learn how to walk away or stay away from drugs and alcohol, or addiction could be in your future.

21–30: Moderate Exposure. Something in your life is hindering your normal development, which makes you want to use or drink. It's best to cut out the usage or drinking before things get out of hand. Get help soon.

31–50: Major Exposure. You are a user or drinker and proud of it. Right now things may seem all good, but they can turn sour any day. Your life is being thrown away each time you use or drink. You may need to check into a facility if things don't change by the end of this book. You could even lose your life before making it to the last chapter. Seek help for your mental health as you start your road to being clean and sober.

Example:

1 Never	2 Sometimes	3 Often	5 Always	Scenario: I have seen my parents use drugs or get drunk.
☐	☐	☐	☒	

Sociological: Friends & Social Networks

1 Never	2 Sometimes	3 Often	5 Always	
☐	☐	☐	☐	I have trouble speaking out loud.
☐	☐	☐	☐	I loose friends or have lost all my friends.
☐	☐	☐	☐	I always listen to my friends when they tell me to use or drink.
☐	☐	☐	☐	I get into arguments with friends over using or drinking.
☐	☐	☐	☐	I seek attention more than any of my friends.
☐	☐	☐	☐	I need to be the center of attention.
☐	☐	☐	☐	My friends use or drink.
☐	☐	☐	☐	When I go party I drink or use.
☐	☐	☐	☐	My friends tempt and encourage me to use or drink.
☐	☐	☐	☐	I have and enjoy drug or alcohol centered entertainment or clothing.

Totals each column				
				Grand Total:

SCORE INTERPRETATION_____

0–10: Low Exposure. Nothing gets to you. You are able to resist even the greatest of temptations. Keep it up but watch out for those negative situations.

11–20: Minimal Exposure. Drinking or using is okay to you when the situation allows. This can be a concern. When friends are drinking, you feel the need to in order to fit in. Be a misfit; walk away from those situations.

21–30: Moderate Exposure. Looking for the party is what you regularly do. You see nothing wrong with it—until you get in trouble, that is. It's time to reflect seriously on your life. Where do you want to be right now? Where do you want to be in the future? Is this usage or drinking going to help you get there? Could you do this during your dream job or during your big moment? If not, you might want to walk away from it all and pursue your dreams.

31–50: Major Exposure. You live a life of risks and spontaneous fun. Your friends are fearful of your next escapade, and your personality screams, "Help me!" Take a long, hard look at yourself in the mirror and see the abuse you have caused. Coincidently, your face is one of the first places where drug and alcohol abuse shows up. If you are unhappy with your life or insecure, now is the time to turn it around. Drop the substances, and go for everlasting peace, joy, a natural high on life, and permanent intoxication by being high on success.

Example:

1	2	3	5	Scenario:
Never	Sometimes	Often	Always	I have seen my parents use drugs or get drunk.
☐	☐	☐	☒	

Environmental: Home, School & Neighborhoods

1	2	3	5	
☐	☐	☐	☐	I see drugs and alcohol sold near my home.
☐	☐	☐	☐	The type of parties I go to always has the drink and the drugs.
☐	☐	☐	☐	I get drugs for alcohol from adults.
☐	☐	☐	☐	I get pressured to use drugs or alcohol at school.
☐	☐	☐	☐	My family provides for all my basic needs (food, shelter, clothing, water).
☐	☐	☐	☐	I spend the night at friend's houses so I can use or drink.
☐	☐	☐	☐	Court is the only thing that makes me stop using or drinking.
☐	☐	☐	☐	I am allowed to use or drink where I currently live.
☐	☐	☐	☐	The people I live with drink and use.
☐	☐	☐	☐	Fears, concerns, and problems where I live cause me to use or drink.

Totals each column				
				Grand Total:

SCORE INTERPRETATION_____

0–10: Low Exposure. You are truly blessed. Stay away from places where drugs and alcohol are served out in the open and you have nothing to worry about.

11–20: Minimal Exposure. Drugs and alcohol are evident in your environment. Begin to look for ways to stay away from these substances. Think of places you can go where there are no drugs and alcohol—the gym, the pool, the park, the lake, the church, and so on.

21–30: Moderate Exposure. Drugs and alcohol are everywhere you look. Your challenge is to ignore what is being served in your environment. You must begin to look at all the negatives as motivation to push you into the positive. Think of the drug addict or the alcoholic in your environment. That person was once you. You have a chance to turn it around.

31–50: Major Exposure. You are probably thinking of your next high or your next drink. You may even be thinking about whom you're going to call right after you indulge your addiction. News flash: people overdose and die of alcohol-related deaths every hour in the United States. Don't be one of them. Repent, which means to turn away forcefully from something that is not pleasing to God.

Example:

1	2	3	5	Scenario:
Never	Sometimes	Often	Always	I have seen my parents use drugs or get drunk.
☐	☐	☐	☒	

Cultural: Family & Traditions

1	2	3	5	
☐	☐	☐	☐	My culture encourages the use of drugs and alcohol.
☐	☐	☐	☐	My culture views drugs and alcohol as our right.
☐	☐	☐	☐	Drugs or alcohol products are my cultures main form of economy.
☐	☐	☐	☐	My culture allows my drug and alcohol usage.
☐	☐	☐	☐	In order to be accepted in my culture you must be an active drinker or user.
☐	☐	☐	☐	When I refuse to use or drink I am rejected by the people of my culture.
☐	☐	☐	☐	Where my culture is from we take pride in our drugs or alcoholic beverages.
☐	☐	☐	☐	My culture is known for its drug or alcohol.
☐	☐	☐	☐	My cultures main representative is known for their drug or alcohol usage.
☐	☐	☐	☐	My culture rejects those whose refuse.

Totals each column				
				Grand Total:

12

SCORE INTERPRETATION

0–10: Low Exposure. Your culture is safe. You have nothing to worry about as long as you do not entertain the thought of using or drinking. Keep your thoughts on what is right, what is noble, and what is true according to the laws of this land.

11–20: Minimal Exposure. Your culture somewhat accepts that behavior, but you know deep in your heart that it is not for you. You have to begin to fight what may be traditional or common with what is best for you. Every time you are confronted by your culture, cling to whatever is noble.

21–30: Moderate Exposure. Your family does it, and your neighbors probably do it. Every gathering is a chance to carry on the legacy. You have to push yourself to stay away from the substance abuse. It may take relocation; it may take you speaking against your culture. You must draw a boundary today. It's for your own health.

31–50: Major Exposure. Drugs and alcohol are life for you. There seems to be no way of escaping them. You have to strategize how you will be able to say no and remain true to your bloodline. The easiest way is to think about your children. Would you want them to be doing even worse drugs and drinking much more than you? What would you say to your children to keep them from turning out like some of your family members?

Example:

1	2	3	5	Scenario:
Never	Sometimes	Often	Always	I have seen my parents use drugs or get drunk.
☐	☐	☐	☒	

Spiritual: Faith & Religious Practices

1	2	3	5	
☐	☐	☐	☐	I pray and read the Bible
☐	☐	☐	☐	I have a spiritual leader who I can speak with
☐	☐	☐	☐	I attend church service
☐	☐	☐	☐	I hear God through (dreams, visions, voice, feelings, etc.)
☐	☐	☐	☐	I feel my drug and alcohol usage is opposite to my spiritual growth.
☐	☐	☐	☐	I search and listen to God for ways out from my drug and alcohol usage.
☐	☐	☐	☐	I use scripture to fight urges to use or drink.
☐	☐	☐	☐	I feel it is wrong to put drugs and alcohol in my body.
☐	☐	☐	☐	I feel God helps me fight my issues with drugs and alcohol.
☐	☐	☐	☐	I pray for God to remove drugs and alcohol from my life.

Totals each column				
				Grand Total:

SCORE INTERPRETATION_____

0–10: Low Exposure: You are standoffish to spirituality. You may be so open-minded to everything that you are closed-minded to spirituality. Try opening up your mind to the possibility that God does exist and that He has been trying to communicate to you. The fact that you are reading this book is proof that He cares for you and that He is seeking an intimate relationship with you. Open your heart and open your mind to something divine.

11–20: Minimal Exposure: God is tugging on your life. You may be so preoccupied with the world that you are forgetting to give your problems up to someone in a higher place. God has the ability to take away the pain, the hurt, the shame, the guilt and the damage you have done to your body. Take a moment to connect with God and pray about these categories in your life.

21–30: Moderate Exposure: Your relationship with God is strong. You know who He is, and He knows you. One thing He does not know is why you treat His vessel the way you do. Do you not know that your body is not your own but is a temple for the Holy Spirit to dwell in you? Take a moment of silence to cast out all uncleanness and all defilement. Ask the Holy Spirit to fill you up and take away your desire for drugs and alcohol.

31–50: Major Exposure: Spend the next few minutes in prayer for yourself, your friends, your family, your environments, and other young people who are reading this book trying to find a way out of their substance abuse.

DAY 2

It's nine o'clock at night, you're at home, the phone buzzes, and just as you were pacing back and forth, perfecting the lie you were about to tell your grandma, you lose your train of thought. Distracted by the text, the made- up thoughts begin to escape your clouded mind. You just rehearsed the factitious account as if writing a five-point speech. "We're gonna catch a movie and then ... I am going to spend the night and then ..." A lie so sophisticated that even the FBI couldn't determine its validity. And you thought you could pull the veil over Grandma's eyes.

It starts with small, undetectable lies to hang with "those friends." You know, the ones who do "those things." These small lies invade your life like ticks on the forest floor—so small yet so deadly. You see, ticks embed their heads into whatever they bite down on, slowly infecting the surrounding area, and then the body becomes diseased. The actions you take grow in your life, keeping you at ease or creating disease.

And then there's "that friend." The one who gets away with it all, the one whose parents are either oblivious or ignorant, but either way, they are encouraging you to partake in their child's misguided "fun."

It's nine o'clock at night, you're at home, the phone buzzes, and just as you were pacing back and forth perfecting the lie you were about to tell your grandma, you read the message: "Whatchu gettin into 2nite?" And you prepare the lie.

It wasn't until you picked up this book and realized the influence friends have on your life. *If every moment is a chance to turn it all around, then every chance is an opportunity to reflect on your choices.* This is your chance. This is your moment of reflection.

It's nine o'clock at night, you're at home, and the phone rings— only this time no one is there to pick it up. You are watching your favorite show, laughing away with Grandma, while thinking to yourself, *another day clean and sober.*

Over the past few years of working with young people, I have discovered the number one cause contributing to youth and substance abuse. It is bad company (friends or social influences) corrupting good character. These influences can cloud judgment, make an unattractive situation appealing, distract youths from dealing with the issues of life, and rob them of their integrity. A simple self-inventory can determine where other factors reside, but for now we will focus on bad company;

"It's natural from the earth. If God didn't want us using it why would he put it here for us?."

"One time won't kill you."
"This will help you relax."

Although these are some of the most popular sayings among substance abusers in the early millennium, we rarely get to see the flip side of their lifestyles. The characters that glamorize these lines remind us of a lot of our close friends. They end up in situations that alter their lives, running into gunfire or becoming so intoxicated that they can't remember where they have been or whom they have been with. In the case of young people ages twelve to seventeen, these characters ultimately hook them into a lifestyle that only 16.2

percent of youths in America are a part of (YRBS, 2011). That means that in our nation, 83.8 percent of youths are not being treated for their substance abuse. Friends, movies, songs, and family do not influence them. That 83.8 percent do the opposite of what they see, hear, and learn from friends. Examine yourself by asking yourself these questions: Who am I listening to? Who do I want to be like? Who am I, not what do I do?

> You must not do as they do in Egypt,
> where you used to live, and you
> must not do as they do in the land
> of Canaan, where I am bringing you.
> Do not follow their practices.
> —Leviticus 18:3

God has great plans for you. God wants you to live a life that represents His glory. But first you must turn away from your sin. Today and each day after, your goal will be to eliminate the threats that damage your ability to stay clean and sober. Here is what successfully clean and sober youth practice:

1. Changing their contact information and deleting negative influences.
2. Making new friends.
3. Seeking support from trusted adults.
4. Schedule tasks during the usual hangout times.
5. Finding small groups or free events to attend.
6. Serving in a ministry during the times they would usually hang out.
7. Meet with an accountability partner (further discussed later in the book).

DAY 3

> Then He who sat on the throne said, "Behold,
> I make all things new." And He said to me,
> "Write for these words are true and faithful.
> **—Revelation 21:5**

Drinking and using drugs took me to a pit. This dark, non-luminous pit had a hard *rock bottom*. After hitting the bottom, the worst of the worst in my abuse, I began to climb out. Once an addicted person starts to climb out of this pit they encounter several stops on their way out the pit to recovery. Today you are going to examine your stage of recovery. Just like stages in life, someone who is addicted to substances undergoes stages or levels of addiction and stages or levels of recovery. The time spent on each stage or level may span a short while or linger for quite some time. While maintaining abstinence from your substance of choice, you may digress or progress on any given day. Whatever the case, successfully clean and sober youth analyze their current stage or level of recovery. Review your self- inventory before moving forward.

STAGES OF RECOVERY

There are two ways to overcome addiction: "By abstinence or by stopping the addictive behavior" (Overcoming *Your Alcohol or Drug Problem* by Dennis C. Daley and G. Alan Marlatt).

STAGES OF RECOVERY

Stage 1: Awareness and Early Acknowledgement

This is the stage when you are aware that this behavior is causing you more harm than good. This is also the stage where you are able to acknowledge to self and others that you have a problem.

Ask yourself these questions: Do I have a problem? Is this substance illegal at this age? Is it causing me to act, feel, and do things that most people wouldn't normally do?

Write in your answers:

_____

_____

_____

_____

Stage 2: Research and Consideration

This is the stage where you begin to examine ways to stop using and you investigate the damages the substance can cause.

Ask yourself these questions: Am I doing all that I can to consider the treatment options? Am I seeking the truth about what this substance can do to my body? What have I done to research and consider my addiction?

Write in your answers:

_____

_____

_____

_____

Stage 3: Exploring Recovery

This is the stage where you begin to call and visit recovery programs. You are taking control of your actions by seeking help. The fact that there is help out there stirs hope in your heart and mind.

Ask yourself these questions: Am I being responsible for my actions? Have I begun to repair the damage I may have done to my body? Am I seeking help?

Write in your answers:

_____

_____

_____

_____

Stage 4: Early Recovery

This is the stage where you begin to abstain from substance abuse. The urges and cravings may be there but you have begun to look toward the future, not toward the past.

Ask yourself these questions: Am I staying away from the addictive behaviors? Have I really stopped my usage? Do I plan to live substance-free?

Write in your answers:

_____

_____

_____

_____

Stage 5: Active Recovery and Maintenance

This is the stage when you can count the days you have abstained, when you know what activities can keep you away from substance abuse. This is the stage where you do what you have to do in order to stay clean and sober.

Ask yourself these questions: Do I want to stay clean and sober? Can I picture a better life for myself? What opportunities will I go for if I am clean and sober?

Write in your answers:

_____

_____

_____

_____

> And do not be conformed to this
> world, but be transformed by
> the renewing of your mind, that
> you may prove what is good and
> acceptable and perfect will of God.
> —Romans 12:2

Now be honest with yourself and write down what stage you are in:

_____

_____

_____

_____

What would be worse than where you currently are?

_____

_____

_____

_____

What things do you have to do to get to the next stage?

_____

_____

_____

_____

How can you start doing those right now?

_____

_____

_____

_____

DAY 4

The game is over, and the habits are exposed. Through self-inventory you have discovered what areas of your life promote substance abuse. Day 2 examined supports and asked you to replace the negative influences with positive influences. Taking a huge step toward the positive requires positive friends who will push you toward your goal of being clean and sober, friends who hold you accountable to the goals you have set for your future. Accountability pushes you when you're slow to change and catches you when you fall from new heights. Accountability is equal to friendship but requires confrontation in order to make change. If your life were explosive like a rocket then accountability would be the afterburners that lift you to your maximum potential beyond the atmosphere. Successfully clean and sober youth have accountability on a regular basis to grow closer to their goal of abstinence by discussing feelings, thoughts, tough times and close calls. Today you will seek out an accountability partner. This person must fit the following criteria:

My accountability partner
* is willing to meet at least once a week;
* is willing to be open and honest with me;

* is willing to pray with me;
* is of good or better conduct than myself; and
* has been clean and sober for at least two years.

With this in mind, think of three friends or close individuals with whom you can be honest. Write their names below:

_____

_____

_____

Out of these three, pick the two who, in your opinion, are most spiritual:

_____

_____

Out of these two, pick the one who has been clean and sober the longest (you may have to call the person to find out):

_____

> Two are better than one, because they have a good return for their labor: If either of them falls down, one can help the other up. But pity anyone who falls and has no one to help them up. Also, if two lie down together, they will keep warm. But how can one keep warm alone? Though one may be overpowered, two can defend themselves. A cord of three strands is not quickly broken.
> —Ecclesiastes 4:9–12

Before approaching this person, ask for God's approval on your choice. Pray that this person will help you confess your struggles and push you to reconcile your wrongs. Pray that they are equipped for the job of being your accountability partner. (Spend some time in prayer now.) Lastly, after prayer, introduce this person to the concept of accountability and see if he would like to continue meeting. Have him or her purchase this book or follow along with you in order to help you quit the drugs or drinking.

DAY 5

> This is what the Lord says: "Stand at the crossroads
> and look; ask for the ancient paths, ask where the
> good way is, and walk in it, and you will find rest for
> your souls. But you said, 'We will not walk in it.'
> —Jeremiah 6:16

Saying NO remains the hardest thing I have to do. Friends still invite me over their homes and ask if I would like wine or other alcoholic beverages. I still run into friends from my past who want me to stop and smoke or use with them. NO remains a constant go to answer in these cases. Successfully clean and sober youth know how that quitting revolves around their ability to say NO. Quitting requires that you drop the old habits and begin the new habits. You may be sitting there thinking, *why should I stop?* Successfully clean and sober youth don't ask *why* they ask *why not*. A simple decision-making process such as weighing the pros and cons can help you figure out what your life might be like if you continue along the path on which you are headed. Essentially, a pro is something that is for you, something constructive, whereas a con is against you and represents something destructive. Take the time to list two sets of pros and cons:

PROS AND CONS

The Pros for Stopping Today

1. Example: Get off probation
2. _____
3. _____
4. _____
5. _____

The Cons for Stopping Today

1. Example: Become a square
2. _____
3. _____
4. _____
5. _____

The Pros for Continuing Another Twenty-Five Years

1. Example: Super fun
2. _____
3. _____
4. _____
5. _____

The Cons for Continuing Another Twenty-Five Years

1. Example: Early death
2. _____
3. _____
4. _____
5. _____

Your challenge today is to share your pros and cons for stopping with your accountability partner, followed by a conversation and prayer about your cons for continuing. Ask this person to support you in achieving some of your pros starting today.

DAY 6

> Let your eyes look straight ahead; fix your gaze directly before you. Give careful thought to the paths for your feet and be steadfast in all your ways. Do not turn to the right or the left; keep your foot from evil.
> **—Proverbs 4:25–27**

He hears the click of his wheels hit the asphalt on a hot ninety-two-degree day in San Diego. As he hops onto his board and begins to push off with his power thrust, his leg is tightly coiled like hair being pressed and curled in a beauty salon. The first kick he lets out is one of pure joy. In solitude for most of the day, dedicated to completing his economics paper by two that afternoon, he says, "That should give me enough time to catch the 936 from Canton Drive to College Avenue, arrive by two thirty, and skate for at leeeeaaaast two hours before I have to get back home." He switches legs and pushes off the asphalt with his left leg. Powered partially by anxiety from his skate injury last week and his need for speed, his heart pounds harder in anticipation of the upcoming curb. You see, to him, curbs aren't just dividers where the sidewalk meets the street; they are unconquered basins with jagged edges, asking brave souls to leap over them.

He hops and ollies, flying at top speed. At this point, everything around him becomes a blur. The wind rushing past his ears becomes his soundtrack for the summer of 2003. As he looks back at the six-inch leap of death also known as the curb, he thinks, *I could have bit it hard,* in reference to the pavement of which he has to make a life-and-death choice of—go for it or bail on a daily basis.

The irony is that he hasn't even begun today's skate session and he's already high. Naturally, that is.

The Sundt definition of a natural high is "any activity, art form, or sport that you love and that makes you feel good inside." The story above alludes to the rush of doing something you love, even in its simplest form. Her heart pounds when she's on stage; he's more relaxed than a La-Z-Boy recliner when he goes fishing; they laugh so hard at each other that they don't even need to drink. Today will be your chance to partake in the delicacy of a natural high.

Take a moment to free write about an activity, art form, or sport that takes you away from all your troubles and all those substances. Make sure to cover these five points in your freewrite:

1. Describe the activity you love.
2. Describe how it makes you feel.
3. Describe what you like most about it.
4. Describe what skill level you want to achieve.
5. Describe how often you would want to get naturally high with this activity if you had the time.

Your challenge today is to share this with your accountability partner and then make time for this activity or art form at least twice a week. Doing activities such as this can help you keep on the right track with your goal of abstaining from substance abuse.

DAY 7

> All of us have become like one who is unclean, and all our righteous acts are like filthy rags; we all shrivel up like a leaf, and like the wind our sins sweep us away.
> —Isaiah 64:6

It was whole new ball game, sophomore year at a four-year university. *I've made it,* I thought. Thinking back to one year prior to my acceptance at San Diego State University, I found myself sitting in a leather recliner talking with my boy Abby about going to college. "It's a distant dream," I told him. He urged me and pushed me to complete the online application, saying, "What do you have to loose, Mark, man?"

When I was a child, my mother would drive past the large campus on the hill that overlooked the valley. There was nothing but tall buildings and bright lights. I would look up out my window and imagine what it would be like to be on the campus of a university, reaching for a higher education.

At age twenty-one, I was a C average student who had yet to dedicate his all toward the achievable. I was a community college veteran, a fourth-year community college freshman. But I had major dreams. Eventually, I would receive that acceptance letter, and eventually I would call San Diego State my campus.

My dreams turned to nightmares as I began my first semester without books, without determination, and without a clue about studying. It was sensory overload; there was fun, girls, pajamas in class, and nonstop parties. I began to lose my faith because of the lust of my flesh and the pride of life. I would predrink and then get drunker and drunker at the various parties, sometimes two or three parties in one night. I eventually started drinking to cope with the shortcomings of my academics. I had bad grades because I drank, and I drank because I had bad grades. Instead of taking care of myself and pulling myself out of my hole, I only dug deeper and deeper. Eventually, classmates and schoolmates began to ask me if I was walking around campus drunk during the middle of day. My reputation for partying overtook my ambition for success. I was addicted to alcohol.

STAGES OF ALCOHOL ADDICTION

The Diagnostic and Statistical Manual of Mental Disorders, Fourth Edition (DSM-IV), has categorized three stages of alcohol addiction:

1. Preoccupation or anticipation
2. Binge drinking or intoxication
3. Withdrawal or negative effect

These are characterized, respectively, by constant cravings and preoccupation with obtaining the substance; using more of the substance than necessary to experience the intoxicating effects; and experiencing tolerance, withdrawal symptoms, and decreased motivation for normal life activities.

Much as I did, some of you are going through intense cravings to get "faded" or cravings for the need to loosen up with a drink. Much of this starts subtly but can lead to much worse complications with your body, your life, and your children's lives. This chain can be stopped by exposing the root of your usage, taking a moment to reflect, share, or write:

1. The first time I drank was ... (share your story). _____

   _____

   _____

   I still do it to this day because ... _____

   _____

   _____

2. Getting drunk helps me to ... _____

   _____

   _____

3. The overall issue that I struggle with is ... (acceptance, confidence, shame, guilt, embarrassment, anger). _____

   _____

   _____

4. Drinking takes that away, which allows me to ... _____

   _____

   _____

Take a moment to pray and forgive yourself for drinking to mask what is really happening. Ask God to come in and deal with your issue listed above. Give it to Him, letting Him know that it is too large for you to hold on to.

DAY 8

> Therefore, since we have been justified through faith, we have peace with God through our Lord Jesus Christ, through whom we have gained access by faith into this grace in which we now stand. And we boast in the hope of the glory of God. Not only so, but we also glory in our sufferings, because we know that suffering produces perseverance; perseverance, character; and character, hope. And hope does not put us to shame, because God's love has been poured out into our hearts through the Holy Spirit, who has been given to us.
> —Romans 5:1–5

RELAPSE IN DETAIL

There is a belief in the behavioral health field that relapse is a stage in recovery, although it is highly debatable. I will provide you with a clear definition and let you decide for yourself if relapse is part of recovery.

WHAT IS RELAPSE?

A relapse is a period or instance of usage after abstaining from a substance. Not to be confused with a "slip." A relapse happens the moment a substance enters back into your body intentionally, whereas a slip is often an unconscious mistake. It is important to note that when you relapse, all your clocks, records, goals, action plans, and treatment plans must be reset and readjusted. Relapse can be discouraging, but you must persevere even in the darkest and most tempting moments.

RELAPSE WARNING SIGNS

Warning signs of relapse include added stress, uncontrollable emotions, environments, and cravings. These warning signs are also called "triggers" because they can set off a huge relapse if they go unaddressed or covered up. A red flag concerning relapse may be when your attitude, thoughts, mood, or behavior toward the substance changes. Once your mind begins to justify (make right) using the substance or drinking the alcohol, you must immediately talk with your accountability partner or a drug and alcohol counselor, as relapse may be creeping up.

> The strongest kids I know are not hindered by the experiences they've gone through. They've turned poison into medicine.
> —Pauline Gordon

DAY 9

Even youths grow tired and weary, and young men stumble and fall; but those who hope in the Lord will renew their strength. They will soar on wings like eagles; they will run and not grow weary, they will walk and not be faint.
—Isaiah 40:30–31

STAGES OF CHANGE

Alex was a hustler. He would sling weed in his community, selling to friends and just about anyone who had the money to buy. His family had a history of being gang involved as well as being heavily involved in the drug culture. Alex was different from the average inner-city youth; he tested very well in the gifted and talented programs. Although Alex was smart, his life circumstances begin to catch up with his academics. Around thirteen years old, he began to hang out with kids who weren't developing their potential but instead were the opposite of who he was. They were cool, they were mature, and they were into more dangerous and illegal activities. This kind of behavior appealed to Alex, so he began to partake in juvenile delinquency.

By seventh grade, Alex had been expelled from school for bringing a knife. At the age of thirteen, Alex faced many problems in his neighborhood, and weapons seemed to be the answer. After being expelled, Alex entered an alternative school program where he was no longer considered gifted and talented. In fact, much of his education was dumbed down. Alex mentions, "I was doing crossword puzzles for classwork and then just playing around on the computer afterward, or we would play football for half of the school day."

After the peer pressure, the unsafe environment, and the dumbing down of his education, Alex began to get involved in the drug life. "I felt so out of place once I got to regular school because I had been around gangstas and potheads for so long that I continued their behaviors once I got there."

Originally, Alex's cousin introduced him to weed and pressured him to smoke. His cousin told him, "You're a little punk if you don't smoke this." So Alex began to smoke. He hated it at first because it hurt his lungs, but then he just began to live with it, and that's what made his life change for the worse.

STAGES OF CHANGE

1. Precontemplation
This is the stage where you are in denial. You don't see your usage as an issue. There is no thought of change; in fact, you are not ready to change and therefore do not even think about changing.

2. Contemplation
In this stage of change, you know you have a problem and you have started to consider quitting. You think about how much better your life would be without the substance.

3. Preparation
This is the stage where you start to tell others that you are planning to quit. You set a date and start to prepare yourself mentally by voicing your plans.

4. Action

In this stage, you have quit or are actively seeking a treatment program in which to detoxify. You begin to learn about yourself and your motivation, and you pick up new techniques for staying clean and sober.

5. Maintenance

This is the stage where you learn who and what to avoid. You actively seek alternatives to drugs and alcohol. Concerned about your progress, you practice and learn more skills on refusing drugs and alcohol as well as managing your emotions and thoughts regarding your use.

6. Termination

In this stage, the desire to use is completely gone. You have gotten rid of your old thoughts of drugs and alcohol, replacing them with new thoughts of growth and change. You are optimistic about your new life and won't allow anything to step in your path toward success.

CHANGE CHALLENGE:

From the list below, circle the items you hope to change after you quit substance abuse.

As a result of my quitting, I hope to change the following:

BIOLOGICAL: self-harm, weight, appearance, hygiene, diseases, infections, skin, hair

PSYCHOLOGICAL: depression, fear, anxiety, anger, suicidal thoughts, low self-esteem

SOCIAL: friendships, family relationships, mentor relationships

ENVIRONMENT: school, grades, hobbies, job, living situation, neighborhood

CULTURAL: respect, trust of my community, representation of my ethnicity, cultural traditions of healthy living

SPIRITUAL: prayer, reading, serving, helping, worshiping

REFLECTION
Write down what stage of change you are in today:

_____

_____

_____

_____

Write down which parts of life you hope to change, and why:

_____

_____

_____

_____

MEDITATION CHALLENGE
Spend a moment visualizing what your life would look like if you were to change those factors circled early. Picture your life changing as a result of your quitting. Perhaps you have saved more money, perhaps you have started a family, or perhaps you gotten your dream job. Anything that comes to your mind, go ahead and meditate on it. Enjoy a preview of your future life.

DAY 10

> And we all, who with unveiled faces contemplate
> the Lord's glory, are being transformed into
> his image with ever-increasing glory, which
> comes from the Lord, who is the Spirit.
> **—2 Corinthians 3:18**

Transformation can be an ugly and scary process. Caterpillars turn into butterflies, earthquakes form mountains and valleys. Volcanoes form new landscapes. These are all forms of transformation. In nature, in order for something to grow, something has to die. Life on our planet now requires the death of something. Just like Earth and its creatures, in order for you to grow, your addiction has to die. In order for you to live, you have to suffocate your addiction. This presents the reality of withdrawal.

Withdrawal is a stage of transformation where the bonding of the substance to your brain begins to recede. Most drugs and alcoholic beverages are chemical in nature or cause chemical reactions in your brain. Upon quitting, the brain chemicals attempt to balance themselves, causing all kinds of distortions and disturbances throughout your body. The following is a chart of withdrawal in which you may be feeling some of these effects this week—but keep on pushing for your change, keep pushing for your sobriety, keep stretching for that life you should be living. The following chart was adapted from *Overcoming Your Alcohol or Drug Problem*.

WITHDRAWAL

ALCOHOL

tremors in the hands, tongue, and eyelids; nausea; vomiting; weakness; sweating; high blood pressure; anxiety; depression; irritability; low blood pressure; delusions; hallucinations; seizures; anger

Days
1–5
Meds
Valium, Librium, Serax

NICOTINE

cravings, drowsiness, gastrointestinal, tension, anxiety, restlessness, oral fixation

Days
no specific duration
Meds
nicotine patch, electronic cigarettes, nicotine nasal sprays

COCAINE AND OTHER STIMULANTS

depressed mood, fatigue, sleep issues

Days
no specific length
Meds
bupropion, mazidol, SSRI antidepressant, baclofen, gabapentin, copycat meds: amphetamine, methxylphenidate, pemoline

OPIATE AND NARCOTIC

runny nose, tearing eyes, dilated pupils, goose bumps, sweating, diarrhea, yawning, fever, insomnia, vomiting

Days
1–14

Meds

methadone, buprenorphine, clonidine

You may need medication if experiencing any of the following:

* You are unable to stay clean and sober for three to six months.
* Treatment does not work after three to six months.
* Your body reacts when you try to quit causing you not to be able to quit.
* Your cravings always get you in the first few hours when you try to quit.
* Your mental or physical health gets worse when you quit.
* You think medication should be in your treatment.

DAY 11

So do not fear, for I am with you; do not be dismayed, for I am your God. I will strengthen you and help you; I will uphold you with my righteous right hand.

—Isaiah 41:10

TRIGGERS, URGES, AND CRAVINGS

I have been in the youth development field for two decades, and the second biggest reason I hear for substance abuse is stress. Managing stressful situations can be tough. Stress unmanaged can trigger urges and cravings to use or drink. Stress can come in the forms of family issues, academic issues, legal issues, financial issues, relationship issues, and depression. This day we will focus on identifying your triggers, urges, and cravings. Your ability to resist substance abuse is based on your ability to choose the best response to life's issues. Stress leads to triggers, triggers lead to urges, urges lead to cravings, and cravings lead to relapse.

Take a moment to circle some of your triggers, urges, and cravings from the list below:

Triggers	Urges	Cravings
stress	events	smells
anger	memories	access
court & tickets	places	boredom

finances	people	desire for
family	paraphernalia	feelings
employment	music	thoughts
depression	movies	
anxiety	media	
relationships		
peer pressure		

Next, using the printout from the link below, track the intensity of your triggers, urges, and cravings since day one of this book. Then share your log with your accountability partner or your counselor.

Daily Cravings Worksheet:
Instructions:
https://www.oxfordclinicalpsych.com/mobile/view/10.1093/
med:psych/9780199334513.001.0001/
med-9780199334513-appendix-10

Blank Sheet: https://www.oxfordclinicalpsych.com/
mobile/view/10.1093/med:psych/9780199334513.001.0001/
med-9780199334513-interactive-pdf-002.pdf

DAY 12

> Do not be anxious about anything, but in
> every situation, by prayer and petition, with
> thanksgiving, present your requests to God.
> —Philippians 4:6

MANAGING YOUR EMOTIONS

> You can't control what happens to you;
> you can only control how you react.
> —Institute for Multicultural Success

Understanding your emotions can be some of the greatest learning moments, but knowing what to do once you recognize them is freedom. Today we will focus on understanding five of your basic emotions: anger, sadness, fear, happiness, and shame.

Take a moment to identify which emotion makes you run to alcohol or drugs and write it here: _____.

_____

_____

_____

_____.

Take a moment to identify which emotion your loved ones feel as a result of your substance abuse, write it here: _____.

_____

_____

_____

_____.

Have you ever felt loneliness, guilt, or hurt? If so, journal about an experience that left you lonely, guilty, or hurt, describing what you did with those feelings.

_____

_____

_____

_____.

Then take the next few hours to write down your emotions. List one emotion every hour on the hour and then write down what that emotion drives you to do. After you are done, write in what you actually did under that emotion.

Example:

Time: 5:00 a.m.   **Emotion:** Bored   **Feelings:** Makes me want to go out and find something to get into. Instead, I will finish my classwork.

6:00 a.m._____

_____

7:00 a.m._____

_____

8:00 a.m._____

_____

9:00 a.m._____

_____

10:00 a.m._____

_____

11:00 a.m._____

_____

12:00 p.m._____

_____

1:00 p.m._____

_____

2:00 p.m._____

_____

3:00 p.m._____

_____

4:00 p.m._____

_____

5:00 p.m._____

_____

6:00 p.m._____

_____

7:00 p.m._____

_____

8:00 p.m._____

_____

10:00 p.m._____

_____

11:00 p.m._____

_____

12:00 a.m._____

_____

1:00 a.m._____

_____

2:00 a.m._____

_____

3:00 a.m._____

_____

DAY 13

> We demolish arguments and every pretension that sets
> itself up against the knowledge of God, and we take
> captive every thought to make it obedient to Christ.
>
> —2 Corinthians 10:5

MANAGING YOUR THOUGHTS

When you feel the urge to use or drink, it's important to picture yourself doing the exact opposite of what you're thinking.

> An important aspect of challenging thoughts
> about substance abuse is not only to visualize
> what one is not going to do but to picture what
> one is going to do as an alternative to using.
>
> —SAMSHA, CYT Series

Pick four out ten ways to take charge of your stray thoughts, use them to stay motivated prompting you to quit:

- ☐ Pray for the strength to control your thoughts and be sure to reread the Scriptures at the top of each day.
- ☐ List unpleasant experiences associated with drinking or using.
- ☐ Distract yourself with other thoughts and tasks.

- ☐ Think of more important things you have to get done.
- ☐ Search the Internet for interesting things.
- ☐ Reinforce your success by reminiscing on why you quit and how you found this book.
- ☐ Review your previous entries in this book since you have started to quit.
- ☐ Focus on the positives for quitting today, which are listed on your pros and cons worksheet.
- ☐ Think of the people in your life who would be disappointed if you kept using.
- ☐ Think of the people in your life who would be hurt if you kept using.
- ☐ If your thoughts are really bad, put off drinking or using for just thirty minutes; chances are you won't even come back to it.
- ☐ Go on a trip away from your current location.
- ☐ Call someone or text someone and strike up a positive conversation.

CHALLENGE

Write down several daily affirmations that will help you focus on your goal of being drug and alcohol free. Take a moment to write each of these on a sticky note or program these into your calendar for a daily reminder.

MY AFFIRMATIONS

I am quitting today because I want ... _____

_____

I am quitting today because I want ... _____

_____

I am quitting today because I want ... _____

_____

I am quitting today because I want ... _____

_____

I am quitting today because I want ... _____

_____

DAY 14

> Keep my commands and you will live; guard my teachings as the apple of your eye. Bind them on your fingers; write them on the tablet of your heart. Say to wisdom, "You are my sister," and to insight, "You are my relative.
> —Proverbs 7:2–4

JOURNALING

Journaling is an insight into your mind; it's a journey less traveled and a destination less seen. Through this journey, you are able to see the path you are walking in, the path you have chosen, and the path you have yet to take. If your life could be picked up and read, this journey would have your entire autobiography and then some! Your task is to write your goals down for each day or week. Plan to write the events of the day, the emotions you are experiencing, and the feelings you are undergoing. This is not a book of pointless memories; rather, it is a book of clues to your identity. Your children should be able to read your journal and understand what it was like to walk in your shoes.

> A journal is a place where we can give expression to the fountain of our heart, where we can unreservedly poor out our passion before the Lord.
> —Donald A. Whitney

Take a moment to review the different ways to journal and then fill in the template below for today.

WAYS TO JOURNAL

1. Devotional _____

3. Prayers _____

8. Free flow_____

4. Word webs_____

2. Inspiration_____

5. Insights_____

6. Poems_____

7. Letters_____

9. Stories _____

10. Chapters _____

11. Hour by hour_____

12. Experiences_____

GAME OVER JOURNAL TEMPLATE

Day, Month, Year _____

_____

Today's Scripture _____

_____

Today's Affirmation _____

_____

My Thoughts _____

_____

DAY 15

> Are not five sparrows sold for two pennies? Yet
> not one of them is forgotten by God. Indeed, the
> very hairs of your head are all numbered. Don't be
> afraid; you are worth more than many sparrows.
> —Luke 12:6–7

SELF-ENCOURAGEMENT

After giving up our childhood home, struggling place to place and being evicted my mother kept the hope of stable housing alive in us by taking us to model homes throughout San Diego and Riverside County. Each model home was staged with room décor for children and fully furnished living rooms, dinning rooms and master bedrooms. Each weekend we would look forward to dreaming, pretending or imagining these places were ours. My sisters would claim the rooms that had two beds, I would always claim the "boys" room that was always decked out in sports, fishing or cars. We would run into this model home and really live there for a few hours on a Sunday or Saturday afternoon. Looking at model homes as a family was our favorite thing to do. Sadly, we never purchased another home but my mother instilled vision in me and encouraged me to pursue something bigger than my current circumstances. By the age of 25 I was closing on my first home, a dream come true but not possible without all those years of envisioning it and encouraging myself to go after my dreams.

Perhaps you were loved as a child. Your parents may have told you things like this: "You are beautiful," "You are smart," and "You are special." Perhaps your parents were the opposite and called you every name in the book, forcing you to think of yourself as less than whole. Sometimes the world does the same. It will tell you that you are on top of the world. It will tell you that you are different, you are special, you are loved. But it can also tell you that you are incomplete, inadequate, stupid, or that you don't measure up to the standard. This is where a positive affirmation or self-encouragement is needed. Presidents, CEOs, professional athletes, and professional entertainers have all mastered the ability to affirm themselves through positive self-talk or self- encouragement. It's what gives them the upper hand on the rest of us. Think about your own situation ... When is the last time you spoke words of encouragement or love to yourself?

Masaru Emoto, a Japanese doctor of alternative medicine, tested the effects of gratitude and positive language on the molecular structure of water. Dr. Emoto exposed the water to written words, pictures, and spoken word as well as music. He then froze the water and photographed the crystals within the water. The results were famous ... Dr. Emoto found that the molecules that underwent exposure to positive thoughts, music, and words grew beautiful crystals, while the molecules that were exposed to negative thoughts and words grew dark, deformed crystals. Emoto's study suggests that positive words, thoughts, and music can create effects down to the molecular level. "If thoughts can do that to water, image what our thoughts can do to us" (From the 2004 film *What the Bleep Do We Know?*).

Best-selling author Laurie Beth Jones shares: "I once went to a seminar where the leader asked, 'How many of you people believes in yourself one hundred percent?' Two people raised their hands. As the leader went further and further down the percentage scale, more and more people raised their hands. The majority of the people in the room believed in themselves 75 percent of the time. The leader then asked, "Why are you afraid to go the other twenty-five percent? What do you think would happen?"

Journal about what your life would be like if you believed in yourself another 25 percent. What opportunities would you take? What kinds of adventures would you get into? Each morning starting tomorrow, make it a point to take two minutes to stare into your mirror and share some encouraging or positive words about yourself as well as a new challenge you will conquer for the day. Then see if your mood or self-esteem begins to change over the course of this week.

DAY 16

FAMILY REBUILDING

How large is the impact of family in our lives? *Huge!* Family Facts shares just a few facts regarding the impact of families. For more details, visit www.familyfacts.org.

* **Emotional:** Compared with peers whose parents are often absent throughout the day, teens whose parents are present when they go to bed, wake up, and come home from school are less likely to experience emotional distress.

* **Self-esteem:** Youths whose parents exhibit love, responsiveness, and involvement tend to have higher levels of self-esteem and internal self-control.

* **Educational:** Students whose parents are more involved with their schooling tend to complete higher levels of education and are more likely to graduate from high school than peers whose parents are not so involved.

* **Behavior:** On average, adolescents whose fathers are more involved in their lives and discuss important decisions with

them exhibit lower levels of aggression and antisocial behavior than peers who experience less paternal involvement.

* **Delinquency (boys):** Adolescents who experience supportive and affectionate relationships with their fathers are less likely to engage in delinquent behavior than peers who do not experience such a relationship.

* **Sexual behavior:** Youths whose parents discuss with them sexual behavior standards are more likely to be abstinent. Also, teenage girls who experience father absence are more likely to become pregnant than girls whose fathers are consistently present.

* **Tobacco use:** On average, adolescents who are strongly connected to their parents and other family members are less likely to smoke cigarettes.

* **Substance abuse:** Compared with other peers, adolescents who report having a positive relationship with their fathers are less likely to smoke, drink alcohol, or use marijuana.

* **Academic achievement:** On average, youths whose fathers engage in leisure and educational activities with them achieve better grades than peers whose fathers spend less time with them.

* Compared to teens who have two or fewer family dinners per week, those who have five or more are at least half as likely to have used tobacco, alcohol, or marijuana. They are also less likely to say they would try these substances in the future or that they have friends who use them.

—The National Center on Addiction and Substance Abuse at Columbia University, 2011

From these statistics, we see that the first twenty years of life are highly affected by family. In fact, your family will affect your entire life. They can directly influence your culture, your values, your beliefs, and your practices. Why is this book stressing the family? Because family is an important aspect of your recovery.

Reconciling with your family starts by fixing your rights and wrongs and can help boost you toward your next stage in recovery. Spending time with your family can also boost your factors for recovery and help navigate your life in the areas mentioned earlier. Imagine growing so much that you enjoy being in the presence of your family, whether they are substance abusers or just plain annoying. Imagine growing so much that you as a parent know exactly what to give your children in order for them not to turn to drugs, drinking, or sex for fulfillment.

In my personal experience with young people, the foster care system can accelerate negative affects regarding the family. I once counseled a youth who had undergone twenty different foster care placements by the age of eleven. Despite all the circumstances, his concept of family and his need for a family were so strong that it transcended all the wrongs he had endured while in custody of his parents. He constantly chased after his family, even in the presence of danger and disappointment. Although his group home family was a manufactured family, he still knew the sense of urgency in reconciling with his true family. They completed him.

The first step in rebuilding family is an apology, followed by acceptance and then a reintroduction. Take a moment to list those in your family with whom you need to reconcile:

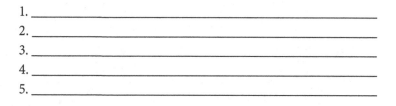

1. _____
2. _____
3. _____
4. _____
5. _____

Begin the process by dropping in to see them or giving them a call to right the wrongs in your relationship with them. Also make it a point to spend at least one day a week developing strong healthy relationships with family. Warning: This may require you to tolerate family members who get on your last nerve ...

DAY 17

> You were taught, with regard to your former way of
> life, to put off your old self, which is being corrupted
> by its deceitful desires; to be made new in the attitude
> of your minds; and to put on the new self, created
> to be like God in true righteousness and holiness.
> —Ephesians 4:22–24

WRITING PROCLAIMS THE NEW YOU

One of the most memorable moments of the twenty-first century had to be the inauguration of America's first black president. It was a major change for a country that has historically had forty-three white commander and chiefs since 1789. It was the beginning of change for a growing country. One important aspect to remember is that change happens over time. When the nation's first black president, Barack Obama, campaigned, he inspired the nation toward change. Barack believed that America could change from a classist, deficit-defiled, arrogant nation to a nation that takes care of its poor, fights for equality, and self sustains its own economy. When he talked about change, it's important to realize that he wasn't shooting for change during the first year of his presidency. He was promising change for future generations. President Obama is a great example of overcoming adversity in the midst of change. You see, change never happens overnight, unless there is divine intervention. Change takes time. Change is a bit of prophecy because change is not promised during current circumstances. Instead, it is realized in the next.

To encourage my young brothers, I often sent letters to mentees who were incarcerated. Young Philip, at nineteen years of age, felt the strain of the natural process of change. Philip had many things going in a positive direction; he had a wonderful girlfriend and a beautiful child, and he was going to trade school while completing his GED. However, Philip was faced with an obstacle. The hustle of street life was calling him. Philip was called to "bust a lick" (a robbery). In the process, he and his crew were caught and Philip faced prison time. In jail, Philip began to reflect on his life and his attitude toward change. Here are his words, written from his cell, where he was caged by concrete and iron bars:

> *Mark my brotha, how have you been? I have been meaning to write you. As of today, I have nine more days till my release. I get out on March 29 [2012] after one last court date. I got a deal for time served at sentencing. So I get out after five months in this hellish place. I've done it all, my friend: smoked, shot messages out, jumped people, and been jumped [in jail]. I have lost it all and got it all back, at least what really matters in life. I have my true love back. I'm going to use all the help and resources you have set up for me, and I'm going to chase this last dream to be a mechanic, take care of my family, and follow God. That old life I was living on the streets, smoking and hanging out with people who were up to no good, got me here, and I almost lost everything, but God has given it all back to me. All I have to do is follow him and I won't ever come back to a place like this, but if I go back to that wrong path, I'll lose it all and end up in prison for years. They gave me a strike and probation. Also, I been a "trustee" for the past two months; that's when I work around the jail doing*

inmate laundry or kitchen and other things. I'm in the kitchen right now; I don't like it, but it beats being on the mainline. I took your advice. I stay quiet and stick to myself. I just work out, read books, and my Bible. I'm in Joshua right now.

My life has changed so much. I found out I got two real friends, and they're from my church so I can hang with them, but all those cats I was doing dirt with or drugs with are out to get me 'cause when we got caught, I told the truth [about] what happened. So I know I am stuck watching my back, but I don't worry. God will protect me. I pray every day and look forward to what you set up for me. I decided to try to be a Jehovah's Witness and have them accept me again, but I'm a Christian, so I will listen to what you have to say 'cause your teaching comes from the Bible, not your opinion, and the Word is the truth. I'm building my testimony. I may even write a book or just share my story like you did. When I heard your story, I knew I wanted you to be my mentor. I could relate a lil, and you were doing bad, but you stopped and became somebody. That's what I want to do—just be someone and do something I love. Also, me and my girl are going to wait till we're married to have sex, and we won't get married unless I have a career and my church accepts me. So it's going to take some time.

Write me before I get out. Hope to hear from you soon. Philip.

Letters to those whom you have hurt can be powerful. Words have the ability to give life and renewal; some people can best observe your dedication and perseverance through your actions, but your dedication and perseverance may be best initiated by your written

71

thoughts. Spend today writing a letter of apology to those you have hurt with your choices or you behavior. Include these things:

* the phrase "I apologize"
* admission of all the wrongs you have ever done to this person
* the phrase "I am seeking your forgiveness"
* a mention that you have forgiven yourself and are planning to move toward a better direction in life
* the plans and steps you are making to change your life
* a concluding prayer

DAY 17

> So I say, walk by the Spirit, and you will
> not gratify the desires of the flesh.
> —Galatians 5:16

REDIRECTING

STAR has currently made its way into the recovery field. It is one of the most prolific lessons I have ever learned. In 2005, I applied to work at a group home in Imperial Beach, California. Having lived in a transitional housing program for former foster youth and homeless teens, I knew exactly how I was going to impact the lives of the children in this group home. I was going to show them a positive male role model who nurtures, cares, teaches, and corrects them in order to make them stronger and more productive citizens. Man, did I learn a lot from them. They made me more nurturing and more caring; they had more influence on me than I did on them. One of the things that really stood out to me in our training for counselors was the STAR method we asked the children to exhibit. STAR involved four phases when confronted with the temptation to lash out, blow up, or lose your cool.

Let us revisit the five basic emotions from earlier. We are taught that we humans have five basic emotions that we attempt to balance throughout our lives: anger, sadness, hurt, shame, and fear. Loneliness, guilt, hurt, and happiness have also been suggested as basic emotions, but for now we will focus on the first five. Here is how the Institution for Multicultural Success defines each emotion:

* **ANGER:** A feeling of power in the gut, followed by a surge of muscle tension in the lower, middle, upper back, and shoulders. Followed by a rush of adrenaline and blood flow throughout the body.

* **SADNESS:** An empty feeling localized in the throat, head, and abdomen, which can manifest into crying. A hallow or light feeling in the upper chest and gut, especially when a deep loss has been experienced or re-lived.

* **HURT:** An ache in the pit of the stomach as if we've been kicked in the gut, plus a feeling of violation, betrayal, or pain.

* **SHAME:** At its deepest level, shame is experienced in the lower gut. It is a feeling of being broken, defective, unworthy, unlovable, stupid, ugly, dirty, awful, bad, evil, crazy, or worthless.

* **FEAR:** Fear is felt in the upper chest and breathing passages. It is a sense of dread and anxiety, and it often spreads throughout the entire body.

STAR aims to override negative reactions in response to your five basic emotions by going through the following phases:

* **STOP:** In the moment of chaos, in the moment you feel you are about to lose control over your body and do something that won't work out for your good or the good of those around you, stop.

* **THINK:** Think about the possible outcomes to your actions: Will this person hurt me? Will I hurt them? Will this

substance make things better or worse? Will I still have to deal with this situation after? What am I attempting to mask by doing this?

* **ASSESS:** Take time to weigh the options and choose the one that allows you to still achieve your goals of recovery or treatment. This is a great time to pray for God to help you make the appropriate choice. Ask the Holy Spirit to take over your thoughts and emotions as you move through the situation.

* **RESPOND:** Respond with the best possible action, knowing that you have weighed the consequences of your actions.

Try using the STAR method today or teaching it to a young person in your life.

DAY 18

MY FUTURE LIFE

Babylonia, one of the most well-known ancient cities among early civilizations, is known for its future plans superseding its purpose. Babili, or the "Gateway to God," as it was known in the late 1800s (BC), before the common era, was an infamous civilization whose people attempted to exalt themselves over all living things on Earth. How would a culture do that? By building a tower for recognition. Like most countries today that have large structural and technological accomplishments, Babili attempted to build a tower that reached into heaven, hence their name "Gateway to God." Scripture says that they disobeyed God by exalting themselves higher than God so that mankind may worship their achievements. They built an enormous tower to make a name for themselves. This plan was not committed to the Lord, nor did it honor him. In fact, the civilization was scattered by God for their wicked hearts, which were set on pride in themselves. Here is the account:

The Tower of Babel

*Now the whole world had one language and a
common speech. As people moved eastward, they
found a plain in Shinar and settled there.*

*They said to each other, "Come, let's make bricks
and bake them thoroughly." They used brick instead
of stone, and tar for mortar. Then they said, "Come,
let us build ourselves a city, with a tower that reaches
to the heavens, so that we may make a name for
ourselves; otherwise we will be scattered over the face
of the whole earth."*

*But the Lord came down to see the city and the
tower the people were building. The Lord said, "If as
one people speaking the same language they have
begun to do this, then nothing they plan to do will
be impossible for them. Come, let us go down and
confuse their language so they will not understand
each other."*

*So the Lord scattered them from there over all the
earth, and they stopped building the city. That is why
it was called Babel—because there the Lord confused
the language of the whole world. From there the Lord
scattered them over the face of the whole earth."*

—Genesis 11:1–9

Babili was attempting to violate the laws set forth by God, which
were to be fruitful and multiply the earth. Instead, they stood still
in one place and attempted to become superior to all others. This
account reflects much of what we do in our lives today. We make
major plans all for our own recognition, and they are not coming
to pass. How many times have you thought of making six figures
for yourself or owning a large money making business or acquiring
and leasing land? It sounds nice, but what good is wealth if you're

not helping those who are less fortunate. What good is recognition if God doesn't recognize you?

Today's challenge is to come up with three goals for your life; each goal should be supported by three steps to get there. The catch is that you have to constantly pray about them, commit them to the Lord, and focus on reaching each of those goals. Here is your goal sheet to fill in:

MY FUTURE GOALS

1. _____

Step 1 (Deadline) _____

Step 2 (Who will help me?) _____

Step 3 (What resources will I need?) _____

2._____

Step 1 (Deadline) _____

Step 2 (Who will help me?) _____

Step 3 (What resources will I need?) _____

3. _____

Step 1 (Deadline) _____

Step 2 (Who will help me?) _____

Step 3 (What resources will I need?) _____

DAY 19

DANGER OR OPPORTUNITY

Every day is a chance to turn it all around; however, you can be so stuck in fear that your opportunities become distant dreams. It's easier to see the danger when you're looking at a risky situation, but it's much better if you take a moment to seek the opportunity in each situation. Seeking the best way out in each situation is called coping. Coping is making the appropriate choice in a situation that can be stressful or in a situation that places you in conflict, where you must choose between danger and opportunity. Today you will take the coping skills test. Please make sure to answer honestly, as if you were placed in each situation at this exact moment.

—Adapted from Jump Start by the Institute
for Multicultural Success

COPING SKILLS

Test Directions:

This test is intended to simulate real-life experiences and determine how well you cope with them. Choose the response that is most gratifying to the person you used to be. If none of these apply, write in what you think would happen. After you finish, compare your answer with the simulated response.

1. **You get in a car knowing that the driver is high. He starts smoking while driving.**
   a. You laugh and enjoy the ride.
   b. You ignore his actions.
   c. You decline the ride.
   d. Your answer: _____

2. **You enter a party, and there is free alcohol ...**
   a. You get in line for some brew.
   b. You try to have a good time without drinking.
   c. You think about leaving.
   d. You leave.
   e. Your answer: _____

3. **Your friends want to steal some alcohol from the store, and they ask you to be the getaway driver.**
   a. You say yes.
   b. You say no.
   c. Your answer: _____

4. **You ditch school to hang out with friends, and someone has a bag of drugs.**
   a. You take a hit.
   b. You try to have a good time without drugs.
   c. You think about leaving.
   d. You leave.
   e. Your answer: _____

5. **Your best friend starts to use crystal meth but thinks it's okay because it's "only on the weekends."**
   a. You agree.
   b. You try not to be associated with him or her.
   c. You stick to your drug of choice, and you two get high together.
   d. You inform the school counselor of your friend's problem.
   e. Your answer: _____

6. **You are walking home after using, and a police officer detains you.**
   a. You try to ditch the drugs.
   b. You try to explain why you appear to be high.
   c. You deny everything.
   d. You run.
   e. Your answer: _____

7. **Your friends bring alcohol to school and drink it on campus; however, they have never been caught.**
   a. You try it only once.
   b. You join them in drinking.
   c. You watch while they drink.
   d. You stay away from them when they have alcohol.
   e. Your answer: _____

8. **Your guardians leave for the weekend, and you are left at home. You discover their alcohol stash.**
   a. You drink a little.
   b. You try to get drunk.
   c. You keep the stash locked away for the weekend.
   d. You call a friend to come hang out with you.
   e. Your answer: _____

9. **You meet someone special and find out later that they use drugs.**
   a. You pretend it's okay.
   b. You join them.
   c. You move on once you find out.
   d. You tell your friend about the effects and try to help them quit.
   e. Your answer: _____

COPING SKILLS TEST RESULTS

1. **You get in a car knowing that the driver is high. He starts smoking while driving.**
   a. You get into a car crash and lose the functioning of your legs.
   b. You get into a car crash and lose the functioning of your legs.
   c. You have made the right decision to walk away.
   d. Your answer: _____

2. **You enter a party, and there is free alcohol.**
   a. The party gets raided, you are detained, and your guardian has to come pick you up from the police department 2am..
   b. You end up drinking, and the party gets raided; your guardian has to come get you at 2am.
   c. You walk around for a while and then leave, but the police detain you outside the house.
   d. Congratulations. You have mastered self-control.
   e. Your answer: _____

3. **Your friends want to steal some alcohol from the store, and they ask you to be the getaway driver.**
   a. Your friends come running out chased by the store manager, who takes down your plate number; the police come and arrest you for robbery.
   b. Your friends leave and get arrested.
   c. Your answer: _____

4. **You ditch school to hang out with friends, and someone has a bag of drugs.**
   a. Your system can't take the drugs. You overdose and nearly die in the hospital.
   b. You end up using, and the drugs are extra strong. You find yourself behind bars.
   c. You end up staying and getting caught ditching by the police.
   d. Good job!
   e. Your answer: _____

5. **Your best friend starts to use crystal meth but thinks it's okay because it's "only on the weekends."**
   a. Your friend becomes addicted and homeless and blames it on you.
   b. Eventually, you try it, become addicted, and have to be hospitalized for treatment.
   c. You decide to try some, and you get hooked.
   d. Your friend calls you a snitch and stops talking to you but gets the help they need.
   e. Your answer: _____

6. **You are walking home after using, and a police officer detains you.**
   a. The officer sees you and tackles you to the ground, injuring your face and leaving you permanently scarred.
   b. You are taken in for questioning in order to find the supplier.
   c. You are arrested and taken to court, where you are given probation and made to pay fines.
   d. The officer tackles you to the ground, injuring your face and leaving you permanently scarred.
   e. Your answer: _____

7. **Your friends bring alcohol to school and drink it on campus; however, they have never been caught.**
   a. You get caught on your way to your next class and get kicked out of the district.
   b. You get drunk after school, wander out into the street, and get hit by a car.
   c. They get caught, and you get expelled for being an accessory.
   d. Excellent choice!
   e. Your answer: _____

8. **Your guardians leave for the weekend, and you are left at home. You discover their alcohol stash.**
   a. You get drunk, and your guardians find out from the neighbor when they get back.
   b. You are successful but are defenseless when someone breaks into the home. You get beat up and robbed.
   c. You made the right choice.
   d. You and your friend start to drink. When you're drunk, your home gets robbed.
   e. Your answer: _____

9. **10. You meet someone special and find out later that he or she uses drugs.**
   a. While in a relationship with them, you become addicted too. The two of you are now serving mandatory prison time for drug-related crimes.
   b. After years of abuse, the two of you are now serving mandatory prison time for drug related crimes.
   c. Good choice.
   d. It doesn't help, but at least you have done what you can.
   e. Your answer: _____

WRAP-UP

Most of the results were negative. The truth is that life can have negative twists and turns. Coping involves weighing the good and the bad, then making the correct choice. How you deal with a situation in a few seconds could affect the rest of your life. Being able to stay away from bad situations determines your success in staying clean and sober. As you can see, there are many paths, but you must decide which one will lead you to your goals.

DAY 20

> For I know the plans I have for you," declares the Lord, "plans to prosper you and not to harm you, plans to give you hope and a future. Then you will call upon me and pray to me, and I will listen to you.
> —Jeremiah 29:11–12

PURPOSE

When you are not walking in your purpose, you can feel it. Your senses begin to dull, and the things that give you joy only exhaust your mind. When you're not waking in your destiny, the sun beats down on your face, attempting to burn back your shell of peace and tranquility. The steps you take on a daily basis become slower, and your momentum is flanked. As if it were cement, you begin to become stuck in the mundane anecdotes of the day as mediocrity plagues your ambition.

But when you are walking in your purpose, each breath is fresh, as if a vine delivered the anointing to your bedside each morning. With power exuding, your light feeds everyone around you, without reservoir your spirit begins to pour out goodness to others. The deserts you crossed each day become meadows with deep green grass. Your future looks brighter than your glow, and you can't help but look ahead, doing so as if you were to run until your journey is over. In your purpose, you find rest. In your purpose, you find meaning. In your purpose, you find eternal life. In your purpose, you find the key to your life and you give love freely to others.

Purpose is your truth; purpose calls you; purpose awaits your response. Eager to embrace your imperfections making you whole, your purpose awaits ...

You are on a mission to find your purpose and capture it! What activity brings you the most joy? What is one thing you would do for free? Purpose is something that if no one paid you to do it, your passion for doing it would overshadow any amount of money. That is where your gifting is. That is where your purpose dwells.

Spend time hunting for your purpose by peeling back all the layers of your life: school, work, family drama, drugs, drinking, and fears. Once you have done that, you will find your purpose. It is at the center of your life.

Find your purpose. Develop your purpose. Live in that purpose.

DAY 21

> Then I acknowledged my sin to you and did not cover
> up my iniquity. I said, "I will confess my transgressions
> to the Lord." And you forgave the guilt of my sin.
> —Psalm 32:5

BURN NOTICE

Getting over your addiction or substance abuse requires that you admit you have a problem and need God to fix it. On this day, you will confess all your abusive moments. What are abusive moments? They are moments when things went bad, you hurt someone, you hurt yourself, you did something wrong to justify your need, or you put yourself or others in danger.

To begin the path of change, follow these steps:

1. Ask God to bring every memory or moment to your mind regarding the situations just mentioned. Allow a few minutes to revisit those situations.
2. Write down each scenario that turned out bad or write down the name of each person or a description of the person who was with you, including anyone who helped you damage your body with that substance or put you in danger.
3. As you think about each item on your list, ask God to help you see your errors clearly.

4. Pray that God will soften your heart and remove all pride so that you may hear Him as you ask for forgiveness. 5. Pray the prayer below for each scenario and each person involved. This may take some time, but be sure to pray in depth regarding each item on your list.

PRAYER:

Father, please forgive me for sinning in Your eyes with my heart and my body. In the name of Jesus Christ, I sever every tie, every chain, and every stronghold associated with _____ (the substance, name, or situation). I am released from this; it no longer has a hold on my soul. I also forgive myself for _____ (the substance, name, or situation). Begin to fill that empty void with Your Spirit now, O God. Create in me a clean heart, renew my spirit, and allow me to move forth in Your will, Father. Let my enemies who set those traps of _____ (the substance, name, or situation) fall in and ensnare themselves. I accept the forgiveness You have given unto me. Make me as new as the morning sun, freeing me from the chains of this beast right now. I plead this all in the name and on the blood of Jesus Christ. Amen.

DAY 22

> We work hard with our own hands. When we are cursed,
> we bless; when we are persecuted, we endure it.
> **—1 Corinthians 4:12**

PRODUCTIVITY

Once you have been freed from drugs and alcohol, your time increases. Days begin to last longer; each hour down to the very minute begins to stretch out in order to accommodate your new lifestyle. The time you spent getting high or looking for your next score or waiting for the function where you would get drunk, now accumulates. It is up to you to spend that time wisely. A wise man once said, "Time is a commodity, Mark. If you never take it, how can you have it?" Time has to be intentionally used on the things that matter in your life. God, family, friends, hobbies, and clean fun are all intentionally good uses for your time; however, some of them are unproductive and can take you away from the important "must do" things in life.

Productivity is an intentional activity that requires dedication, focus, and time. Productivity is a subcategory of time. Productivity says that when you have a down moment, you will dedicate your time to doing something that produces the fruit of accomplishment or you will spend your time doing something that benefits others. Productivity is also something you do in your downtime that pushes toward your goals. I have talked with young people all over, and distractions seem to be the number one hindrance of productivity. In fact, distractions are the opposite of productivity. Distractions are time consuming, and they often leave no changes or no lasting effects on your goals in life.

PRODUCTIVITY IDENTIFICATION

You are applying for jobs and going on a job hunt. It's nine o'clock on a Saturday morning. Take a moment to prioritize the following activities as you begin your day:

D = distraction
P = productive

_____ checking your e-mail
_____ answering your e-mail
_____ posting in your social media
_____ cleaning the house
_____ completing your daily reading
_____ talking on the phone with a friend
_____ printing your resume
_____ talking with your sibling
_____ folding clothes
_____ showering and brushing your teeth
_____ texting your friend back from last night

Getting a sense of what is important is a great skill. The easiest way to think of what's a distraction and what's productive is to think about your goal as each of these things come across your mind. Try it again, this time thinking of the goal—job *hunt*—*before* marking your answers.

D = distraction

P = productive

_____ checking your e-mail

_____ answering your e-mail

_____ posting in your social media

_____ cleaning the house

_____ completing your daily reading

_____ talking on the phone with a friend

_____ printing your resume

_____ talking with your sibling

_____ folding clothes

_____ showering and brushing your teeth

_____ texting your friend back from last night

If you see more Ps, you are on the right track. If you see more Ds, you have to concentrate on getting to the task at hand rather than thinking about what you could be doing. Think about what you should be doing rather than what you could be doing.

DAY 23

> For they mouth empty, boastful words and, by
> appealing to the lustful desires of the flesh, they
> entice people who are just escaping from those who
> live in error. They promise them freedom, while they
> themselves are slaves of depravity—for "people
> are slaves to whatever has mastered them."
>
> **—2 Peter 2:18–19**

PEER PRESSURE

Back to our friend Alex the hustler. As you may remember, Alex grew up in a gang environment. His family was full of gansters. He was intelligent but chose to disengage his book smarts and reengage his street smarts. Alex saw what the cool guys were doing and decided to do it too. Alex began to smoke weed due to his friends, and then he was selling in no time. His home became the local kick-it spot, where weed was free and "high times" were the only times. Alex shared the following:

> I started going from different friends all over the
> place. I started getting into problems with my mom,
> but my mom loved me. One day I would be expelled,
> and then the next day she would buy me a bike.
> Eventually, I quit the weed. I started playing football
> in my sophomore year. I loved it. We practiced a lot,

twice a day sometimes. It was keeping me busy, just playing sports and running hard. It was fun until I started hanging out with another crowd.

I got kicked off the team because I started smoking weed and hanging out again. At that time, I was ditching, going to school late, and missing first period. I started ditching more, and eventually I only went to school for third period. I was pretty much just not going. Then we would find new spots, and I would only come to school for lunch. We got more and more supply. Every month, things kept getting worse and worse. My mom was upset with me 'cause I was rebellious. I didn't want to listen, and I would say stuff like, "This is my life!" At the same time, I started to watch myself bring my girlfriend down with me too. Then everybody around went down too. I just had so much supply that everyone wanted to be around me. I didn't see it, but I was just dragging everybody down with me, you know?"

Peer pressure is a strenuous and continuous activity that makes you feel accepted by others. Peer pressure can be positive or negative. The reason it is so effective is because peer pressure is human nature. Humans are hardwired to be relational. Basically, we were made to want to fit in. When you're in adolescence, you struggle to identify the group where you want to fit in. In the case of Alex, he had several groups to choose from: drugs and hustling, academics, or sports. As you can see, he gave up two for one. The entire time, he knew it was wrong. Some of you are just like Alex. You know what you are doing, you know it breaks your parents' hearts, and you know it is setting you back—yet you still do it.

WHY GIVE IN TO PEER PRESSURE?

Take a moment to think about when you first came out of the womb. Most of you were born natural, drug-free and alcohol-free. As a newborn, you didn't need an ounce of drugs; you didn't need a bottle full of alcohol. You were born natural; you lived a natural life and had a natural high, so why would you want to do something completely opposite? Think about your dreams and goals in life. Does using or drinking promote any of that? Does it push you closer to your goal? Then why are you doing it?

Take a moment to "STAR" (stop, think, assess, and respond) to the questions above. Also take a moment to write about the positive peer pressures you could say yes to. Write your answers below:

DAY 24

> Therefore do not be partners with them. For you were
> once darkness, but now you are light in the Lord. Live
> as children of light (for the fruit of the light consists
> in all goodness, righteousness and truth) and find out
> what pleases the Lord. Have nothing to do with the
> fruitless deeds of darkness, but rather expose them.
> **—Ephesians 5:7–11**

PARTY TIME: SOBER FUN, CLEAN FUN

"Sober fun" sounds like a foreign term, doesn't it? The first time I heard the term was my sophomore year in college at San Diego State. At a party, I was talking with two young ladies I knew pretty well. I had my red cup in one hand and my drink in the other (notice: two hands were full of alcohol). We were talking about something funny and goofy as usual, and then I asked them, "Do ya'll want some drank?" I lifted my bottle up in the air with the cool arm, like I was a bass fisherman holding the catch of the day. They replied; "No, we're having sober fun!" I did not know how to respond. They'd rejected my international peace sign of sharing the brew. It caught me off guard. Suddenly, the pint of Smirnoff I had clutched in my arm began to look like a giant five-gallon water jug. The room got empty (in my mind), and for the first moment, I felt my subconscious began to think. I thought about "sober fun." I thought about being rejected by these two girls I respected and had drunk with before. The wheels began to turn in my head as I thought about "sober fun" and how embarrassed I was about my drinking problem.

SOBER FUN CHALLENGE

Your challenge today, should you choose to accept it, is to give the following survey to twelve random people outside of your class. Tell them you have been asked to complete an anonymous survey regarding substance abuse. You may not assist them in answering in any way. If they don't know how to respond, you may only repeat the question. Keep a tally of each of their answers. Journal about your thoughts from their answers when you're done.

GAME OVER SUBSTANCE ABUSE SURVEY

1. Do you like to drink? Yes _____ No _____

2. Are you under twenty-one? YYes _____ No _____

3. In your opinion, is drinking fun? Yes _____ No _____

4. Do you think that getting drunk is fun? Yes _____ No _____

5. Do you feel that alcohol causes you to lose control over your body? Yes _____ No _____

6. Do you believe that alcohol causes you to lose control over your mind? Yes _____ No _____

7. In your opinion, are you a better person when you drink or get drunk? Yes _____ No _____

8. Do you think that drinking helps you fit in?
    Yes _____ No _____

9. If you never got drunk again, would you fit in with your friends? Yes _____ No _____

10. Do you think you can have fun without drinking?
    Yes _____ No _____

11. Can you go to a party and not drink and still have fun?
    Yes _____ No _____

12. Do you think that people who kill other people in drunk driving accidents deserve their sentences? Yes _____ No _____

13. In your opinion, do you think domestic violence due to alcohol abuse is fun? Yes _____ No _____

14. Do you believe that it is okay to sleep with someone who is too drunk to say no? Yes _____ No _____

15. What do you think "sober fun" is?
    a. A board game_____
    b. Playing beer pong _____
    c. Not drinking at a party _____
    d. Dancing off your buzz _____

DAY 25

> Therefore, my dear brothers and sisters, stand firm. Let nothing move you. Always give yourselves fully to the work of the Lord, because you know that your labor in the Lord is not in vain.
> —1 Corinthians 15:58

SERVING OTHERS

In 2012, I attended a volunteer training at my home church in San Diego, California, and realized how much joy serving others can give you. When you're coming down off an addiction and want to feel the highs that are associated with using or you want to feel the fulfillment that is associated with the drink, you can get the same feeling, and then some, from serving people. I was told at this training that there are four elements to serving others: love, preparation, service, and commitment. Out of these four elements, anyone can experience fulfillment and a natural high.

LOVE: Love is shown through your service and received from your service. Those whom you choose to help will express their gratitude with smiles and hugs, maybe even a thank you. Immediately after serving someone, you may begin to feel a tingling feeling in your chest. Don't be afraid—it's just love that you're feeling. Not erotic love but brotherly love. Human love.

PREPARATION: Service takes preparation, preparation builds anticipation, and anticipation leads to excitement. Serving others can be an adrenaline rush as you begin to build up to your service event.

SERVICE: The act of serving provides human interaction, a necessity for most people. This is the kind of interaction where you are giving your time and not expecting anything in return. Service says that I care more about others than I do myself in this moment.

COMMITMENT: Commitment allows you to put your hand to the plow and then watch the harvest as it is reaped. Commitment sees you through the entire process start to finish. The feelings of accomplishment are far greater than the feelings of failure associated with substance abuse.

> People don't care how much you
> know but know how much you care.
> — Theodore Roosevelt

SERVING CHALLENGE

Serving others says, "I will sacrifice my own needs to reach yours." It's not payback; it is paying it forward.

Your challenge is to serve someone else today. It doesn't matter if it's helping someone carry a water jug, opening a door, or serving sandwiches to the homeless. Take a few minutes out of your day to bring a special moment to another person's life. Remember, you are doing this for the Lord, not for yourself. Serve Him well and journal about your experience. Serving may be something you want to do on a monthly basis, if not more.

Service Journal Entry

Date: _____

Location: _____

Experience: _____

_____

_____

_____

Insights: _____

_____

_____

_____

DAY 26

> But he said to me, "My grace is sufficient for
> you, for my power is made perfect in weakness.
> " Therefore I will boast all the more gladly about
> my weaknesses, so that Christ's power may rest
> on me. That is why, for Christ's sake, I delight in
> weaknesses, in insults, in hardships, in persecutions,
> in difficulties. For when I am weak, then I am strong.
> —2 Corinthians 12:9- 10

FIGHTING FAILURE

I received my first F in the third grade. I will never forget it. For half of the entire year, I turned in no homework. I just gave up on the prospect of completing my work. Each day my teacher would collect homework, and when I did show up with the paperwork in my hand, it only had my name on it and maybe the first couple of questions, which I was able to crank out while waiting outside to be let into the class.

As the school year went on, my teacher called my mom in for parent-teacher conferences, and I knew I was going to get an earful, maybe even a whipping. My mother was known for cursing out office staff whenever my sisters got beat up or teased at school, so immediately I began to think of her cursing out my favorite teacher. I cried hard for her not to come to school and embarrass me. Well, she came to parent-teacher conference night, and to my surprise, she was very upset that her only son was receiving a failing grade at such a young age.

Struggling to find out what the problem was, my teacher began to ask me questions during their conference time. I shrugged my shoulders a lot and hid behind my mom. I finally blurted out, "I don't want to do homework!"

Mr. Harris, my third-grade teacher, placed both hands on my shoulder sternly and said, "Mark, there're going to be things in life you don't want to do but you have to." I thought about my home life, my after-school life. I was running from bullies and getting beaten up daily. At home, I was being abused by visitors and guests. I wanted to tell him that he had no idea what I was dealing with, but I recognized something in his message, something that would echo throughout my life. "There're going to be things in life that you don't want to do but you have to."

I want to share that same message with you. The difference between success and failure is your quitting. Your walking away. Your doing something wrong and leaving it wrong instead of correcting your mistake. Failure happens when you're not doing what you are supposed to do for that season in your life. Since then, I have failed at many things; however, I have never given up. I failed at sports, I failed algebra (several times), I have failed my family, I have failed myself, I have failed friends, I have failed bosses, and I have failed God.

The greatest moments within these failures are the moments when you realize that you made a mistake. When you figure that out, admit it and grab the eraser. Then begin to replace that mistake with a correct move. That's when failure becomes a learning moment, when failure turns to success.

The first time around, I may have dropped the ball, but the second or third time around, I knew exactly where to hit it! I now know the ins and the outs, and I know exactly what not to do.

FAILURE CHALLENGE

Today begin to see your failures as successes by first writing out ten or more mistakes and failures you have made. Second, write how those failures made you feel about yourself. Third, write what you learned *not* to do in a similar situation. Read your list of things not to do while praying about changing the way you complete the tasks of life.

FAILURES AND LESSONS

Failure: Example: Dropped out of high school Lesson: Example: Get help and tutoring next time

FAILURES AND LESSONS

Failure:_____

Lesson:_____

Failure:_____

Lesson:_____

Failure:_____

Lesson:_____

Failure:_____

Lesson:_____

Failure:_____

Lesson:_____

Failure:_____

Lesson:_____

Failure:_____

Lesson:_____

Failure:_____

Lesson:_____

Failure:_____

Lesson:_____

Failure:_____

Lesson:_____

Failure:_____

Lesson:_____

DAY 27

> I know your deeds, your love and faith,
> your service and perseverance, and that you
> are now doing more than you did at first.
> —Revelation 2:19

PERSEVERANCE

Earlier we spoke of Alex, who was a smart, athletic teen who grew up in a not-so-positive environment and eventually gave in to the lifestyle of drugs, alcohol, and delinquency. Alex shared the following:

> *I didn't see it, but I was just dragging everybody down with me, you know? I ended up on probation, and I then found out I got my girl pregnant. Then I got sent to another continuation school, all in the process of a month. That all happened, and it was for the better because I started thinking,* All right, this is where [I] change for the better. *So then I started looking for jobs, and it was hard. I ended up getting a job seven months later. My girl was seven months pregnant, and I was stressing out. My mom was supportive the whole time, even through all that went on. The probation thing ... I hated it, but to this*

day, I think that's the best thing that ever happened to me. I was talking about it with my mom, and if it weren't for probation, I wouldn't have done it for myself or for anybody.

As I started growing, I started paying more attention in school. I wasn't getting stuck out in space anymore. Going to a smaller school gave me more help and a lot of "You're doing great." It encouraged me to go to college. I got a bunch of opportunities to take college classes in high school.

It went from all bad, who I was hanging with, making decisions that were bad, messing up, having fun partying, and smoking ... At times, I was in the same alley for five hours, doing the same thing with the same people, never changing. Today I could say [that] those were the days. I miss those days; I can never hang out like that anymore. I went from finding myself to being a man, and because I am still young, I'm having problems with my baby's mom. I could be partying, but instead I am handling mines. To me, being a man is more important than sleeping around and doing drugs 'cause you know it's all about my son now. My mom didn't do it to me or even my dad, so I was lucky to have that. I am not going to have my son go through that.

It's hard being in a relationship, but at the end of the day, it's worth it. You get to see your son smile and your girl smile, and it's all worth it, them showing you they care even when no one else does. You just gotta play your cards right every day.

I started thinking, All right, this is where I change for the better.

Perseverance makes a huge difference in life. I once read a memorable quote: "The greater the obstacle, the more glory in overcoming it." Perseverance is the principle that says you will push past any obstacle to reach your goal. Find out what is standing in between you and your goals and then move it out of your way. Alex faced his obstacles early in life, but he recognized that there is a fundamental process of change in all created things. He realized that change is possible and that it takes a daily walk with change in order to make things happen. Alex now sees the glory in his daily walk with change. He was awarded several scholarships to college in 2012, and he plans to attend a community college for his first two years and then obtain a transfer guarantee to a four-year university, studying mechanical engineering.

DAY 28

> The fear of the Lord is the beginning of knowledge,
> but fools despise wisdom and instruction.
> —Proverbs 1:7

EDUCATION

Today's opening verse says that fools despise wisdom and instruction. How many of you have friends who hate school or who aren't open to learning new things? I would go so far as to say that this verse is speaking about them. Education is so fundamental in running a society, and you cannot escape the fact that education provides higher pay and more job stability. In fact, the U.S. Department of Education has assembled the information below:

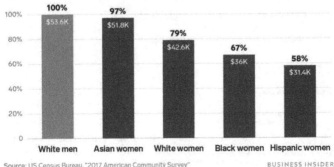

Women's annual earnings compared to white men's

White men	Asian women	White women	Black women	Hispanic women
100%	97%	79%	67%	58%
$53.6K	$51.8K	$42.6K	$36K	$31.4K

Source: US Census Bureau, "2017 American Community Survey"

BUSINESS INSIDER

Mark Black

As American women continue to advance as far as equal rights within the workforce, their annual income has begun to rise. Gender equality seems to be imminent for our future generations. However, income and job stability still seems to revolve around education in America.

Furthermore, the Bureau of Labor Statistics states, "College graduates earn more and are more likely to be employed of their lifetimes than high school graduates." So why is school so important? While earnings are important, so is civilization and the advancement or development of human potential. Schooling provides you with an advanced or developed view of this world. Specialties, certificates, credentials, and degrees are all types of advancements given from school. If society is not educated, then how will we advance? Someone has to learn, someone has to teach, and someone has to share, and someone must receive. You could be that person to learn, share, teach, and receive. Below is a chart representing your earning potential—just an added bonus to acquiring knowledge. At what level would you like to be?

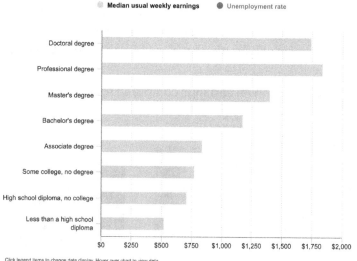

Median weekly earnings and unemployment rate by educational attainment, 2017

DAY 29

FINANCIAL FREEDOM

I would like to share five principles I learned that have helped me to be financially successful: budget, give, pay, save, and spend.

BUDGET: A budget is a forecast or a prediction of what you will do with your money. It may also be called stewarding. Budgeting helps you focus on the bigger picture rather than on the dollars themselves.

GIVE: From time to time, something in us urges us to help those in need. If you are religious, you may give at your local church and associated gatherings. Giving is usually returned. I have often found that when God tells us to give to someone or something, He usually provides much more in return than we gave.

PAY: After budgeting and giving, it is time to pay the bills! I was once at a 450 credit rating (highest risk). I was unapproved for credit cards, bank accounts, and loans. It was so challenging. It wasn't until I incorporated paying back debtors into my monthly budget that

I was able to be financially free. I paid off court fees, got warrants removed, and increased my credit score from 450 to somewhere in the 700s (no risk) because I repaid my debtors.

SAVE: For some people, saving comes naturally; the rest of us need a goal for saving. You can save for a car, a trip to Europe, or that expensive piece of clothing you have always wanted. The point is to get in a habit of putting away money for a rainy day.

SPEND: Spending is the easy part. Spending according to your budget is the hard part. Set aside some spending money each month. Why work so hard if you can't enjoy the fruits of your labor? Spending often comes first for some people, so it may take some practice to spend last. Try these simple guidelines, and watch your debt decrease and your bank account increase!

Visit www.markblack.org for links to budgeting worksheets

DAY 30

> Now, brothers and sisters, I want to remind you of the gospel I preached to you, which you received and on which you have taken your stand. By this gospel you are saved, if you hold firmly to the word I preached to you. Otherwise, you have believed in vain. For what I received I passed on to you as of first importance: that Christ died for our sins according to the Scriptures, that He was buried, that He was raised on the third day according to the Scriptures ...
> ---1 Corinthians 15:1-4

THE GOOD NEWS

Imagine that you have just committed a crime. You are arrested at noon. You are booked, fingerprinted, and made to take a mug shot. You are immediately taken to trial, and based on the evidence presented, you are found guilty. The judge knows and the jury knows exactly what happened. They not only have you on tape, but they also have a written confession from you. To your displeasure, the judge begins to render the guilty verdict. Before he can finish saying the word, though, the court doors are kicked open. Everyone looks to the back of the court. The doors swing open, and a bright light is shining from behind a figure. He walks straight down the aisle and directly to the judge, carrying a briefcase full of money to pay your million-dollar bail. He approaches the judge and bailiff. "I command the release of this person," he proclaims over the court. His gesture is granted. Then He walks over to the bailiff and grabs the keys to your handcuffs. He reaches down to unlock the cuffs on your wrist. As He unlocks the cuffs, all you can say is, "You saved me." He escorts you out of the court to make sure that you make it back to freedom. Then, to insure that justice is served, He returns to the court and stretches out His wrists. He is handcuffed and taken to trial for your crime. There's nothing you can do to reverse this death sentence. He has committed Himself to paying for your crime, even to the point of death.

All have sinned and fallen short of the glory of God. God knows it, and you know it. If you have ever broken any of the laws of God or the Ten Commandments, then you are guilty and have been sentenced to death—eternal separation from all that is good and from God Himself. The good news is that although God is completely just in sentencing you to death, He also loves you more than you can comprehend. He loves you so much that before your trial, He put on flesh to become the ransom for what you have done. God sent His Son, Jesus Christ, to pay for your crime. As a result, if you accept Jesus Christ, the Holy Spirit of God will live in you. He will guide and speak to you on your journey through life. There is nothing you can do because it was determined by God the judge, Holy Spirit the jury, and Jesus Christ the ransom.

Because of Jesus' sacrifice, everyone now has access to this ransom. Because Jesus lived the perfect life, something no other human could do, He became the perfect sacrifice. In exchange for His clean, sinless life, God's justice has been satisfied. Someone has paid the cost for your crimes. All you have to do is accept it, get up, turn around, and walk away from your crimes.

Now is the moment to get up out of that courtroom and walk with Jesus Christ. Now is the moment to accept His love and grace in your life. Give it all up. Throw your hands up and say, "God, there is nothing left for me here. Father, forgive me for my crimes against You. I accept Jesus Christ as my Lord and Savior, and I ask the Holy Spirit to fill my life."

Spend a few moments talking with God. Write down or share everything He tells you or everything that is in your heart and mind regarding His love, grace, and mercy for you.

YOUR DAY

Congratulations and welcome to the beginning of your new life! This is your day. Take a moment to write the end of this booklet according to your life. You finish the story ...

Today's Date: ___/___/___

Day 31
Scripture of the Day

_____

_____

_____

_____

_____

_____

_____

_____

_____

_____

A Short Personal Story

_____

_____

_____

_____

_____

_____

_____

Lessons Learned

_____

_____

_____

_____

_____

_____

How I Plan to Share This with Someone in Need

_____

_____

_____

_____

_____

_____

CONCLUSION

The game is over! Congratulations on reaching your goal of thirty-one days. Some of you were successful at staying clean and sober and some of you weren't, but the point is that you have accomplished the journey of one. You have examined your friends, your family life, your physical state, your mind, your emotions, and your connection with God as you have successfully made it to the end of this manual.

Go out and be great! Go out and continue to strive for a substance abuse–free lifestyle. Share what you have learned with another person who may or may not be struggling with substance abuse. The sky is the limit, so never stop reaching!

I would love to hear from you. Please share your experience with *Game Over* via e-mail by visiting the author's website at www.markblack.org.

ABOUT THE AUTHOR

MARK BLACK is an extraordinary young man and an inspiring speaker. He was recognized for the 2011 Up and Coming Leadership Award in behavioral health by the National Council for Community Behavioral Healthcare (Washington, DC). Mark has been in the youth  development field for more than a decade, coaching and counseling young people in a variety of settings, including high schools, youth camps, faith-based organizations, and nonprofit organizations. He has also counseled and mentored severely emotionally disturbed, system-involved, and at-risk youth.

With his example of overcoming challenges and creating success, he provides inspiration and insight to both youth and adults. Mark has contributed to developing numerous character development and leadership training courses, reaching and teaching thousands of youths and adults per year in youth development and leadership skills. As an accomplished speaker, Mark has spoken for programs and conferences throughout California on topics relating to youth issues. In addition to his numerous accomplishments, Mark coaches track and field, volunteers as a ministry leader, and has served as a mentor for the Foster Youth Mentor Program of San Diego County.